LOVE, POETRY

(L'amour la poésie)

TITLES from BLACK WIDOW PRESS

Translation Series

Chanson Dada: Selected Poems by Tristan Tzara
translated & edited by Lee Harwood

Approximate Man & Other Writings by Tristan Tzara
translated & edited by Mary Ann Caws

Poems of Andre Breton: A Bilingual Anthology
translated & edited by by Jean-Pierre Cauvin and Mary Ann Caws

Last Love Poems of Paul Eluard
translated with an introduction by Marilyn Kallet

Capital of Pain by Paul Eluard
translated by Mary Ann Caws, Patricia Terry, and Nancy Kline

Love, Poetry (L'amour la poésie) by Paul Eluard
translated with an introduction by Stuart Kendall

The Sea & Other Poems by Guillevic
translated by Patricia Terry
with an introduction by Monique Chefdor
(forthcoming)

Essential Poems & Writings of Robert Desnos: A Bilingual Anthology
edited by Mary Ann Caws
(forthcoming)

Essential Poems & Writings of Joyce Mansour: A Bilingual Anthology
translated with an introduction by Serge Gavronsky
(forthcoming)

Eyeseas (Les Ziaux) by Raymond Queneau
translated with an introduction by Daniela Hurezanu & Stephen Kessler
(forthcoming)

Modern Poetry Series

An Alchemist with One Eye on Fire
Clayton Eshleman

Archaic Design
Clayton Eshleman
(forthcoming)

Backscatter
John Olson
(forthcoming)

New Poet Series

Signal from Draco: Poems of Mebane Robertson
(forthcoming)

www.blackwidowpress.com

LOVE, POETRY

(L'amour la poésie)

PAUL ELUARD

translated with
an introduction by

STUART KENDALL

BLACK
WIDOW
PRESS

BOSTON, MASS.

LOVE, POETRY
Paul Eluard

Black Widow Press edition, March 2007

English language translation & introduction © 2006 by Stuart Kendall
L'amour la poésie © Editions Gallimard, Paris, 1929

cover photo: Paul Eluard, 1934 © 2007 Man Ray Trust / Artists Rights Society (ARS), New York / ADAGP, Paris.

Black Widow Press is an imprint of Commonwealth Books, Inc., Boston.
Joseph S. Phillips, Publisher.

All Black Widow Press books are printed on acid-free paper and put into sewn and glued bindings

Black Widow Press
www.blackwidowpress.com

ISBN-13: 978-0-9768449-7-6
ISBN-10: 0-9768449-7-4

Library of Congress Cataloging-in-Publication Data

Eluard, Paul, 1895-1952.
   [Amour la poesie. English & French]
   Love, poetry = L'amour la poésie / Paul Eluard ; translated with an introduction by Stuart Kendall.
      p. cm.
   ISBN 978-0-9768449-7-6 (alk. paper)
   I. Kendall, Stuart. II. Title.

   PQ2609.L75A713 2007
   843'.912—dc22

                                                                       2007003770

Prepress production by Windhaven Press (www.windhaven.com)
Printed by Thomson-Shore
Printed in the United States

10 9 8 7 6 5 4 3 2 1

This translation is dedicated to Bill Minor,
poet and humanitarian

———————————————

contents

All the Names of the World

Bread is more useful than poetry. But love in the complete sense of the term, the human sense of love-passion, is no more useful than poetry.

—Eluard, *The Future of Poetry*

When Editions Gallimard published *Love, Poetry* in 1929, the book's success secured Paul Eluard's reputation as perhaps the greatest poet of his immediate generation, the generation that came of age in coincidence with the First World War.[1]

Eluard dedicated the book to his first wife, his first love, Gala. The poet had given Gala her name when the two first met, as adolescents just before the war. Gala's real name, in the Russian from which she came, was Elena Dmitrievna Diakonova. The young man also renamed himself in this same moment: assuming his grandmother's maiden name, Eluard, in place of his own original last name, Grindel. Renamed, the poet and his beloved were reborn in love.

---

[1] The final two sections, both entitled "Knowledge Forbidden," had been published for the first time the previous year.

Paul and Gala met in Switzerland in 1913 while both were patients at the Clavadel sanatorium near Davos. Both suffered from tuberculosis and they established an immediate and intensely powerful bond. The first poem in *Love, Poetry*, and indeed the entirety of the first part of the book, is believed to be a reflection of their meeting.[2] At the time, Eluard was also in the process of discovering modern poetry (Baudelaire, Whitman, Rimbaud, Lautréamont: books he could not read in school) and his own vocation as a poet. Gala encouraged him and he attached himself to her as her "disciple."[3] Gala did not write but she had a hunger for life and lived passionately. She tutored Eluard in pleasure and he came alive in her hands. The feeling, apparently, was mutual. In *Love, Poetry*, the poet describes it simply, for both of them: "With a single caress/ I make you shine in all of your brilliance."[4]

The patients returned to their parents' homes the following year and announced their plans to marry. World War One complicated the liaison without dampening it. Eluard spent 1915 and much of 1916 enduring the horrors of the front but managed to marry Gala while on a three-day leave in Paris in 1917. Their daughter, Cécile, was born the following year. Shortly thereafter, Eluard's *Poèmes pour la Paix* (1918) led to his friendships with Jean Paulhan and, through Paulhan, with André Breton, Philippe Soupault and Louis Aragon. These were the days of *Littérature*, of Dadaist outrage and experimentation. Tristan Tzara's presence in Paris kindled the rage of these disaffected and war weary young men into a fire that would consume their time. By the early 1920s, the destructive urge had given way to a creative one and Surrealism was born when the Dadaists began to explain the nonsensical products of their cultural and aesthetic criticism with the sense of psychoanalysis.

André Breton had been a medical student before being a Dadaist and he

2 Luc Decaunes, *Paul Eluard* (Editions Subervie, 1964) 15.
3 Cf. Lucien Scheler, "Preface" xvi, in Paul Eluard, *Oeuvres complètes* (Gallimard, Pléiade, 1968).
4 Firstly, XVII.

had already discovered Freud. Freud's then only recently developed theory of an unconscious realm of the mind and his methods for acquiring access to that realm shocked those who were dedicated to the Western episteme and theory of subjectivity. Breton and his friends, however, greeted Freud's theories with the enthusiasm of explorers in an earlier age catching sight of maps of hitherto unknown lands. The mental landscape of Europe had been devastated by the war, its ideals and icons shattered. Freud's theory refashioned that landscape, replacing the ravaged real with a dark, unconscious, ultimately unknowable double. His thought revealed the mythic content of everyday life and the primitivism in the heart of a barbarous civilization. It revealed the bourgeois war mongers, the stuffed shirts who lead the land, as savages. For Freud, sexuality, in its various phases and myriad forms, served as the central figure and prime mover in both individual life and culture as a whole: Eros, in other words, as animator of everything; a sentiment ripe for poetic extrapolation.

Freudian theory provides not only a new model of mind and culture; it provides a means of accessing and exploring that mind and, for the Surrealists, a means of cultural renewal. Psychoanalytic theory explains the significance of myths, dreams, and slips of the tongue, and psychoanalytic method provides a means of decoding these things. Surrealism transformed that method into a means of creating art. Dreams could be transcribed; dream imagery could be painted; slips of the tongue could be provoked through random word association, automatic writing, and games like the exquisite corpse.

Surrealism, in short, took psychoanalysis off the couch and into culture. The Surrealists transformed Freud's therapeutic method and means of personal and cultural analysis into a means of personal and cultural creation. Their works—including *Love, Poetry*—often betray this dual origin and purpose: to analyze and document psychological phenomena while simultaneously provoking and extending the psychoanalytically inspired, sexualized ideal state that they describe. They are both documents of desire and descriptions of an ideal state. Surrealist works may be judged as art objects but they ultimately testify more to an ethos than to an aesthetic.

Surrealism is a lifestyle: its products fragments of a new world and way of living.

Breton and his friends—Eluard among the foremost and earliest of them—styled themselves as "specialists in revolt" whose purpose was to extend the fundamental liberties available to the men and women of their time. They intended to reveal the arbitrary and ridiculous nature of local and contemporary customs of restrained behavior, and to awaken and renew the realm of the imagination, personally and culturally, feeding the soul of their era a diet of irrational thoughts and images. They did this through manifestos and statements, through a journal, *La Révolution surréaliste*, through publications from both small and large presses, through paintings and sculptures, and through films and theatrical productions. Surrealism thus had an impact on all of the arts and, importantly, on the thought of its time.

The Surrealist revolution was ultimately a revolution in desire and in the imagination, and an attempt therein to rethink the origin and nature of reality. In Surrealism, dreams stood alongside and on equal footing with reality; desires were viewed as the root of the real. For Eluard, this philosophy had already proven to have the substance of fact. His adult life effectively began when he met and fell in love with Gala. Her desires and his desire for her constituted the entire truth of his world. She provided both the vision and the frame of his imaginative thought.

The same year Eluard published *Love, Poetry*, the Surrealist group issued its famously defamatory *Second Manifesto*, which summarily expelled, libeled or explained the previous expulsion of traitors to the cause including Robert Desnos, Antonin Artaud, Georges Limbour, André Masson, Philippe Soupault, Roger Vitrac, Pierre Naville, Georges Ribemont-Dessaignes, and Francis Picabia. The expulsions in most cases hinged on questions of social and political revolution, definitions of dialectical materialism, and of the role of art in society. In its sophomore *Manifesto* the group closed ranks, summarized the gains and losses of its first five years, and prepared to set out again from the gates of its dream. It set the stage for a new journal, *Le Surréalisme au service de la Révolution*, and established an agenda for the group and its new adherents: Salvador Dali, Alberto Giacometti, René Magritte, and René Char most promising among them.

A similar tumult marked Eluard's personal life at the time. Unsurprisingly for a relationship begun so young and animated with such pervasive intensity, Eluard and Gala's relationship was also a complex and tempestuous one. André Breton and the rest of the Surrealist group officially adhered to an ideal of monogamous purity in sexual matters, and publicly scorned deviants from this rule. But Gala had greater needs than could be met by any single partner. Eluard, for his part, was not averse to sharing her charms. Thus the painter Max Ernst had a long and intimate relationship with Gala. Despite Eluard's openness, the complexities of his life—lived at the limits of personal freedom—eventually took their toll. In 1924, Eluard fled from his family, from his boring day job, and, most importantly, from Gala. He embarked upon a trip around the world. Eight months later he wired Gala from Saigon, asking her to retrieve him. Max Ernst accompanied her on this mission and Eluard accommodated the ménage, throwing himself even more fully into the life and thought of the then nascent Surrealist movement upon his return.

Five years later, after the first heroic phase of Surrealist activity, and only months after he published *Love, Poetry*, Eluard met and fell in love with Maria Benz. The depth of his attachment can be read in his act of giving her a new name: Nusch. Gala had begun an affair with Salvador Dali, whom she later married, the previous year. Though Eluard and Gala would continue to remain close and occasionally intimate for years to come, both moved on to relationships that in many ways were more satisfying to each partner than their intense adolescent love had been. *Love, Poetry* can thus be read in light of the imminent collapse of the passionate relationship it chronicles. (Eluard's later love poetry is collected in his *Last Love Poems*.[5])

Love, Poetry, then, appeared at a portentous moment in Eluard's own life and in the evolution of Surrealism. Whereas Eluard's previous extended collection of verse, *Capital of Pain* (1926), appeared in coincidence with

---

[5] Paul Eluard, *Last Love Poems*, trans. Marilyn Kallet (Black Widow Press, 2006).

the first few energetic, indeed exuberant years of Surrealist experimentation, *Love, Poetry* (1929) coincides both historically and technically with
the true masterpieces of Surrealist literature: Breton's *Le Surréalisme et la
peinture* and *Nadja* (both 1928), Philippe Soupault's *Les Dernières Nuits
de Paris* (1928), René Crevel's *Babylone* (1927), and Louis Aragon's *Traité
du Style* (1928), to name only a few of the most significant. In these years
and works, the writers in the group managed to harness the methods of
objective chance, automatic writing and dream transcription, to trim them
of their early excesses, and to produce the works for which they would
primarily be remembered. Eluard's *Capital of Pain* is undoubtedly a more
dazzling volume than *Love, Poetry*, but the latter is in many ways more moving and, ultimately, more satisfying as an integrated artistic experience of
motive, vision, and principle.

Love, of course, has long been an essential theme of the lyric form of
poetry. It is perhaps *the* essential theme. From Sappho and the *Song of
Songs* in the ancient world, to the poetry of the Troubadours and Petrarch
at the beginning of the Renaissance, to the writings of the Romantics and of
Baudelaire at the birth of the Industrial and Modern eras, love has been the
central topic of the lyric form. In love poetry, the lyric self contemplates its
relationship with another being, it discovers its limits through the presence
and absence of the beloved, and discovers both communities—the community of lovers—and concrete reality—in the stark contrast between mere
matter and the animate flesh of the beloved. The beloved may stand in for
the supreme deity, though such a substitution is not necessary. (Conversely,
the symbolic presence of the deity may legitimate love poetry in cultural
moments which forbid overt reference to the pleasures of the flesh.) All
that is necessary is that the lyric self encounter and contemplate its meaning
and its limits and that this encounter be heightened as it is in both love and
in the language of poetry.

Another useful perspective on the lyric form comes from Nietzsche, who
famously contrasts the sensibility which generates lyrics with that which
creates epics. For Nietzsche, the lyric sensibility and form is essentially

subjective, emotional and involved, musical and "Dionysian" in its disorder and excess. The epic on the other hand is objective, dreamy and detached, built of clear images contemplated with "Apollonian" distance. The lyric sense is essentially personal while the epic is essentially, one might say, political. In Nietzsche's reading, Greek culture—and his thought on this point is derived from an analysis of Greek culture—managed to fuse these two sensibilities and styles in the art of tragic drama, an art of musical poetry in performance which reveals the personal drama behind and within political problems. In the twentieth century, as we have seen, the Surrealists sought a similar fusion, a fusion of art and life, of the personal and the political, of subjectivity and objectivity, of love and language. The Surrealists took their dreams for realities and their documents—the precipitates of those dreams—for their desires. *Love, Poetry* is both the poetic product of love and a provocation for its reader, a push into the world of dreams and desires that it describes. To read *Love, Poetry*, one must enter into its dream logic, and find oneself lost in its labyrinth of veils.

The dual nature of the work—as product and instigation—proposes an aesthetic challenge to the reader: What, after all, is real? What is dream? What is a mere flight of imaginative fancy? And what is grounded in material fact? In his preface to Eluard's *Capital of Pain*, André Breton wrote, "To be or not to be—we are just beginning to see that *that* is not the question."[6] *Love, Poetry* too continues to keep this question in suspense. Indeed, Eluard's Surrealist verse always challenges any theory of truth based on correspondences, any division of its contents into fact or fantasy, any simple logic. Its images and their relationships, one to another, are intentionally and aggressively non-rational.

When these poems do occasionally possess a narrative, it has the logic of a dream. Its elements and perspectives don't quite connect. Its meaning is unclear. More often, the poems capture scenes or fragments of scenes, images from dreams or day-dreams, fleetingly glimpsed and sparely stated:

---

6   André Breton, *Break of Day*, trans. Mark Polizzotti and Mary Ann Caws (University of Nebraska Press, 1999) 40.

all that matters of a moment. One does not fall in love with the entirety of
a group sitting around a table, one gazes into another's eyes, and at that
moment no one else matters.

The poems can be read as transcriptions from a lover's bedside note-
book. They do not aspire to completion, to the presentation of complete
worlds or bodies, the images here are not distillates from which one might
deduce a satisfying and seamless whole. Rather, the poems and the bodies
they describe are intentionally fragmented, magnified or otherwise dispro-
portionate forms. In questions of desire only the object of desire, potentially
only a fragment of that object, gathers the entire force of one's interest:
a lover's fallen scarf returned gently to her shoulder. Nothing else matters
and everything else recedes into the background. Distance in these images
or scenes acts as a cue to mystery, and mystery—the suspense of clear relationships, clear meanings—a cue to the reader's imagination. These poems
demand our participation in the construction of their meaning and they
deny any satisfactory conclusion to that participation. The book, as Eluard
says in his dedication, is without end.

Restated in Nietzsche's terms, these poems are the products of Eluard's
poetic subjectivity, inspired by his love for Gala, but they are the distanced
and dreamy, and thereby objectified records of that subjectivity. The poet
presents them to the reader for the reader to animate and ultimately possess on his or her own. Without the supplemental work of our imagination,
these words and works are meaningless.

Love inspires *Love, Poetry*: Gala's love for life and for Eluard, Eluard's
love for Gala, Eluard's love of poetry, and the gift that poetic language offers
both its writer and its reader. This relationship, or rather these relationships,
are clearly reciprocal and reciprocally inspirational. "I love so much that I
no longer know/ which of us is absent."[7] We share the poet's love through
his love poetry and this poetry offers itself—as vehicle and extension—to
our love. Would we love without love songs, without love poetry?

---

[7] Firstly, XXII.

Love is of necessity a transformative experience for all parties involved. This may be an adolescent vision of love, but it is also a classic one—invented by the Troubadour poets—and more satisfyingly complete than any other. Is a love that leaves us untouched and independent worth the name? In both the classic model and Eluard's love poetry, love opens a world of clarity, of light within darkness. It reveals what has been hidden, and, like dawn, remakes the entirety of our world in the process.

> Her eyes are towers of light
> under the face of her nudity.
>
> On the transparent surface
> returning thoughts
> cancel deaf words.
>
> She effaces every image
> She bewilders love and its stubborn shadows
> She loves—she loves to forget herself

—Firstly, II

Eluard's poems circle the scene of love. They are inspired by the beloved who is loving and who they love. In them these subjectivities meet, as do the words and images that both capture and convey them. Love poetry is a poetry of paradox: of the speech of a lover's silence, of the mirror that is a lover's gaze, of the living dream figure, of the presence that is in no way distinct from an absence, the self that is the other in love. "Hear me," the lover says, "I speak for those men who quiet themselves best."[8] "My dreams are clear and perpetual/ in this world."[9] The Freudian inspiration and methods of Surrealist writing find their perfect subject matter in love

---

[8] Second Nature, XI.
[9] Firstly, VIII.

poetry, where fantasy and fact commingle in the illusions of love. "I enclose myself within my love, I dream," Eluard writes elsewhere.[10]

Along similar lines, Surrealist thought pushes Baudelaire's dream of symbolic correspondences beyond the limits of the dream. When imagination and dream stand alongside reality, synaesthesia has become complete. Any fetish may stand in for any object of desire. As Eluard puts it in *The Future of Poetry*: "Everything is comparable to everything else, everything finds its echo, its reason, its resemblance, its opposition, its evolution everywhere else. And this evolution is infinite."[11] The verse that results from this faith is not written as a search for adequate metaphors nor as a careful articulation of limited links among images, objects and ideas.

> Mouths gourmands of colors
> and the kisses that draw them
> flame leaf languorous water
> a wing holds them in its palm
> a laugh astounds them.

> —Firstly, XVI

The mouth here fulfills its aesthetic function: the faculty of taste. But the mouth tastes colors, and thereby becomes a vehicle for color and much else. The verse condenses the meanings and associations of the pictured object: the redness of lips, the whiteness of teeth, the function of taste, the desire for kisses, laughter. And the kiss here is both anticipated and aflame, fiery and languorous, flighty, held and beheld. The laugh affects the lips and the bodies connected to those lips.

Eluard's poetry is a poetry of the gaze. The gaze it deploys is that of consciousness, gazing inward in dreams, reveries, and imagination, and it is

---

[10] Eluard, *Au défaut du silence* (1925) in Eluard, *Oeuvres complètes*, vol. 1 (Gallimard, Pléiade, 1968) 165.

[11] Eluard, *Avenir de la poésie* (1937) in Eluard, *Oeuvres complètes*, vol. 1 (Gallimard, Pléiade, 1968) 527.

that of the eye, gazing outward, seeking visual confirmation in the world of dreams and inspiration for dreams in the world of reality. This is a remarkable shift in the history of subjectivity: a shift which inserts the distance required for sight between the self and self-consciousness. It is a distance implied but not required by Freud's division of psyche into superego, ego and "it," the id. The third section of *Love, Poetry* is entitled "As an Image": it greets the "birth of images," but the whole of the work pursues this same emphasis, process and goal.

Eluard's writing ultimately remains beholden to its images: his is an art of description rather than one of narration. He is less interested in states of consciousness than in the images that traverse that consciousness. The images make the states visible, but they do not presume to explain or exhaust them. As he says, "to see is to understand, to judge, to deform, to compare, to forget, or to forget oneself, to be or to disappear."[12] Eluard in this way is very much a poet of surfaces and his work will have its legacy in the writings of the New Novelists, the next generation in French letters.

Unlike that of the New Novelists, however, Eluard's poesis often mistakes the word for the image and both for the flesh. This is of course the great mystery and mistake of Surrealism and of symbolic consciousness in general. How can the word or image be made flesh? What is the root and repose of meaning? Poetry is cosmogonic when it ventures to explain such things.

In the poetry of the Troubadours and of Dante, the flesh receded before the rising spirit, the mark of divinity, which was, for them, the true value of a being. Immediately thereafter, though, Petrarch began a new tradition in Western literature and culture by lingering too lovingly over the details and delights of the flesh. He too nevertheless still fell to the side of spirit when it came to divining the root of transcendent meaning. Six centuries later, the Surrealists inherited this tradition at its end, in the time of the death of god. They inherited a poetics of transcendence in a culture without transcendence and they took it upon themselves to remake the reality of

---

[12] Eluard, *Avenir de la poésie* (1937) in Eluard, *Oeuvres complètes*, vol. 1 (Gallimard, Pléiade, 1968) 526.

that world, replacing the divinities of the past with the dreams and desires of today. For Eluard, "every caress, whether of the body or of language, is sacred."[13] In his synaesthetic delirium, Eluard perceives the world in the body of his beloved, his beloved in the words and images of his poetry, and truth value in the fruit of his imagination. This trope and intellectual gambit requires a careful redefinition of materiality itself and explains the vitriol of the *Second Manifesto*.

With all of this in mind, it is important to emphasize the extent to which—despite its translucent surfaces and ephemeral lightness—Eluard's poetry is a poetry of earthy and physical bodies: "It is with your mouth/ and in the condensation of our kisses/ that we are together."[14] As Eluard explains in *The Future of Poetry*: "Poetry will only become flesh and blood once it has become reciprocal. This reciprocity is entirely a function of the equality of happiness among men."[15] The Surrealist revolution in thought is a revolution in the reality of imagination but it is one that solicits and requires the equal participation of every reader. The reciprocal inspiration at the heart of this fantasy is universal in intent, if not in actual practice. The impetus is at the origins of love and of love poetry as well as of politics and social ethics: Eluard phrased it most eloquently in a startling question: "Which of us invented the other?"[16] The first part of *Love, Poetry* ends sentimentally on this point: "It had to be important that a face/ answers to all the names of the world."[17]

In the years immediately following the publication of *Love, Poetry*, Eluard wrote *Ralentir travaux* with André Breton and René Char and *L'Immaculée conception* with Breton (both 1930), as well as celebrated books like *La Vie*

---

[13] Eluard, quoted in Raymond Jean, *Paul Eluard par lui-même* (Editions de Seuil, 1968) 43.

[14] Firstly, XXVII.

[15] Eluard, *Avenir de la poésie* (1937) in Eluard, *Oeuvres complètes*, vol. 1 (Gallimard, Pléiade, 1968) 526.

[16] Eluard, *Au défaut du silence* (1925) in Eluard, *Oeuvres complètes*, vol. 1 (Gallimard, Pléiade, 1968) 165.

[17] Firstly, XXIX.

immédiate (1932) but his style of the era had been established in the earlier
works and it would not change until his life did.

In 1938, André Breton met Leon Trotsky in his Mexican exile and voiced
support for the embattled figure. Eluard did not approve as he was himself
drifting back into solidarity with the Communist party. The ensuing dis-
agreement ended twenty years of friendship and collaboration between the
two men. Thereafter Eluard's life and work—particularly after 1942 when
he joined the underground forces of resistance in occupied France—were
linked to the struggle for equality among the oppressed, a struggle Eluard
found and fought within the confines of the Communist party. In keeping
with the nature of this struggle, Eluard stripped his style of its opacities,
its obscurities, its flights of fancy, and redirected some of its vigor into an
accessible moral didacticism. Much of his later work retains its power only
when one recalls the context in which it was written: poems published and
disseminated by the French government in exile, dropped as leaflets by the
R.A.F.: inspiration for an oppressed people.

Today, *Love, Poetry* is as unknown to Anglophone readers as Eluard's work
in general (this is its first appearance in the English language). *Love, Poetry*
is unknown in part, I believe, because the shift Eluard and the Surrealists
effected in our sensibility has become so pervasive. They fought to establish
a world in which the perspectives of every individual, whether based on
fact or fantasy, would outweigh the received wisdom of the community as
a whole. A world wherein dreams and reality stand on equal footing. And
we live in that world. The origins of such a world hardly matter to the
dreamers who inhabit it. Eluard's work, in other words, had its effect, but
the work itself did not linger. Like all catalysts, it achieved its ends and was
gone. Nevertheless, any contemporary love lyric written in simple and direct
language without recourse to complex formal devices (meter, traditional
form) owes a debt—whether acknowledged or, more likely, not—to Eluard.

Love, Poetry is also unknown in part because its methods are so simple
and its message so direct. While Eluard's images may often be startling and
startlingly memorable, and while his language may be both accessible and

moving, that very accessibility contributes to Eluard's lack of acknowledge-ment among Anglophone readers and writers. Like Pablo Neruda, Paul Eluard is and always has been a poet for people, for readers, for lovers, rather than a poet for the classroom or literary conference. One does not marvel at Eluard's technical virtuosity, at his audacity. One is moved, that is all.

Finally, Eluard is unknown in this country, undoubtedly, due to his affil-iation with the Communist party during the final decade of his life. For Eluard, the Communist party spoke for common men and women, for people who work for a living, and for people oppressed by political forces beyond their control (at that time, for people oppressed by the Nazis who occupied France). This may be a naïve vision of the Communist cause but at the time it was a noble one and it reveals Eluard's lifelong and essential concern, to protect and extend the freedoms of common men and women, not just in his country but everywhere around the globe.

Upon Eluard's death in 1953, Europe and the world mourned the loss of one the great poets of the age, one of the great voices of resistance to tyranny: French schoolchildren still memorize Eluard's "Liberté." On our shores, McCarthyism and the Cold War silenced any potentially similar lamentation.

Paul Eluard thus remains, to English language readers, one of the great unknown immortals of twentieth-century letters. This aura of mystery is, however, not entirely unfortunate. It allows each of today's readers to come to and appreciate Eluard's work with and for the freshness that is its true nature and greatest gift.

Stuart Kendall
Lexington, 2006

A Note on the Translation

My friend Bill Minor asked me to translate Eluard's *L'Amour La Poésie* more than a decade ago. And I did so. Michelle Kendall participated in that early draft of the book, which I then sent to Bill in response to his request.

I also sent the draft out to some publishers. Over the next few years I discovered how difficult it is to publish a book of poetry in translation, even a book by an author as well known as Paul Eluard and as enjoyable as *Love, Poetry*. Several publishers whose lists include writings by other Surrealist writers, one of whom had a series in Modernist writing, rejected the book claiming that they simply did not publish poetry no matter how closely affiliated it may be with the other titles in their list. The publishers who do publish poetry tend to specialize in contemporary American poetry or British or Canadian poetry, not in poetry in translation. The response from the few who do publish poetry in translation was uniform: yes, Eluard is a great and important poet, and yes, we love his work and would love to publish it, but regrettably our list is full for years to come and we simply cannot publish Eluard. While almost everyone admitted that Eluard made a significant contribution to twentieth century letters, several publishers spoke of their mandate to promote lesser known works or undiscovered talents rather than the work of well known writers. Ironically, this was at a time when only one volume of Eluard's selected poetry was available in translation: Eluard himself had become an undiscovered talent. The two main publishers of mass market paperback editions of classics in translation also passed on this collection because it is protected by copyright law.

Frustrated with the rejections—and with the state of publishing in general—I put the manuscript in a proverbial drawer every few years, only to rediscover it shortly thereafter and send it out once again. With each new effort, I made changes to the translation, some small, some very large. Twice over the past ten years I have entirely retranslated the work, starting afresh each time. Each time too I sent the new draft to Bill for his comments, which he offered with enthusiasm. Occasionally he felt that the previous draft of a particular poem had been more successful than the subsequent one. Other times he suggested changes, small or large. He has in short been involved in this translation from the very beginning and for this reason I dedicate it to him and to his love of Eluard and of love poetry.

I would also like to thank Joseph Phillips, the publisher of Black Widow Press, for his interest in this project and for his straightforward professionalism in its regard. His passionate and partisan approach to publishing is a breath of fresh air in our politically correct corporate marketplace. Mark Polizzotti and Marilyn Kallet too offered significant encouragement and insight into this project at crucial stages.

Finally, Vanessa Corrêa should be mentioned here as she keeps my faltering faith in beauty and that mobile army of metaphors—truth—alive. She offers Surrealist proof that dreams can be shared.

L'AMOUR LA POÉSIE

à Gala
ce livre sans fin.

LOVE, POETRY

To Gala,
This book without end.

Premièrement

Firstly

I

A haute voix
L'amour agile se leva
Avec de si brillants éclats
Que dans son grenier le cerveau
Eut peur de tout avouer.

A haute voix
Tous les corbeaux du sang couvrirent
La mémoire d'autres naissances
Puis renversés dans lumière
L'avenir roué de baisers.

Injustice impossible un seul être est au monde
L'amour choisit l'amour sans changer de visage.

I

Aloud
agile love arose
in such brilliant bursts
that the mind in its loft
was afraid to admit everything.

Aloud
all the ravens of the blood
covered the memory of other births
then astonished in light
the future exhausted with kisses.

Impossible injustice a single being is in the world
love chooses love without changing its face.

II

Ses yeux sont des tours de lumière
Sous le front de sa nudité.

A fleur de transparence
Les retours de pensées
Annulent les mots qui sont sourds.

Elle efface toutes les images
Elle éblouit l'amour et ses ombres rétives
Elle aime—elle aime à s'oublier.

II

Her eyes are towers of light
under the face of her nudity.

On the transparent surface
returning thoughts
cancel deaf words.

She effaces every image
She bewilders love and its stubborn shadows
She loves—she loves to forget herself.

III

Les représentants tout-puissants du désir
Des yeux graves nouveau-nés
Pour supprimer la lumière
L'arc de tes seins tendu par un aveugle
Qui se souvient de tes mains
Ta faible chevelure
Est dans le fleuve ignorant de ta tête
Caresses au fil de la peau

Et ta bouche qui se tait
Peut prouver l'impossible.

III

The all-powerful representatives of desire
newborn serious eyes
to suppress the light
the curve of your breasts held by a blind man
who remembers your hands
your soft hair
is in the unknowing river of your head
caresses on the stream of skin

And your mouth that silences itself
can speak for the impossible.

IV

Je te l'ai dit pour les nuages
Je te l'ai dit pour l'arbre de la mer
Pour chaque vague pour les oiseaux dans les feuilles
Pour les cailloux du bruit
Pour les mains familières
Pour l'œil qui devient visage ou paysage
Et le sommeil lui rend le ciel de sa couleur
Pour toute la nuit bue
Pour la grille des routes
Pour la fenêtre ouverte pour un front découvert
Je te l'ai dit pour tes pensées pour tes paroles
Toute caresse toute confiance se survivent.

IV

I told you for the clouds
I told you for the sea tree
for each wave for the birds in the leaves
for pebbles of noise
for the familiar hands
for the eye that becomes a face or a landscape
and the sleep that renders the sky from its color
for the entire drunken night
for the grid of the roads
for the open window for an uncovered face
I told you for your thoughts for your words
every caress every confidence endures.

V

Plus c'était un baiser
Moins les mains sur les yeux
Les halos de la lumière
Aux lèvres de l'horizon
Et des tourbillons de sang
Qui se livraient au silence.

V

More a kiss
than hands over eyes
halos of light
on the lips of the horizon
and cyclones of blood
surrendered to silence.

VI

Toi la seule et j'entends les herbes de ton rire
Toi c'est ta tête qui t'enlève
Et du haut des dangers de mort
Sur les globes brouillés de la pluie des vallées
Sous la lumière lourde sous le ciel de terre
Tu enfantes la chute.

Les oiseaux ne sont plus un abri suffisant
Ni la paresse ni la fatigue
Le souvenir des bois et des ruisseaux fragiles
Au matin des caprices
Au matin des caresses visibles
Au grand matin de l'absence la chute.
Les barques de tes yeux s'égarent
Dans la dentelle des disparitions
Le gouffre est dévoilé aux autres de l'éteindre
Les ombres que tu crées n'ont pas droit à la nuit.

VI

You alone and I hear the grain of your laugh
your head carries you off
and from the height of mortal danger
under the valley's bustling rain
under the heavy light under the earth's sky
you bear the fall.

The birds no longer find shelter
nor idleness nor fatigue
the memory of the woods nor fragile brooks
in the morning of whimsy
in the morning of visible caresses
in the grand morning of absence the fall.
The barks of your eyes lose themselves
in the lace of disappearance
the gulf is unveiled for others to extinguish
the shadows you create have no right to the night.

VII

La terre est bleue comme une orange
Jamais une erreur les mots ne mentent pas
Ils ne vous donnent plus à chanter
Au tour des baisers de s'entendre
Les fous et les amours
Elle sa bouche d'alliance
Tous les secrets tous les sourires
Et quels vêtements d'indulgence
A la croire toute nue.

Les guêpes fleurissent vert
L'aube se passe autour du cou
Un collier de fenêtres
Des ailes couvrent les feuilles
Tu as toutes les joies solaires
Tout le soleil sur la terre
Sur les chemins de ta beauté.

VII

The earth is blue like an orange
faultless words don't lie
they give you no more reason to sing
it's the kisses' turn to understand
madmen and lovers
blocked union
all the secrets all the smiles
and such indulgent clothes
completely naked to faith.

Wasps flowered green
dawn passes around your neck
a necklace of windows
wings cover leaves
you have all the solar joys
all the sun on earth
on the paths of your beauty.

VIII

Mon amour pour avoir figuré mes desires
Mis tes lèvres au ciel de tes mots comme un astre
Tes baisers dans la nuit vivante
Et le sillage de tes bras autour de moi
Comme une flamme en signe de conquête
Mes rêves sont au monde
Clairs et perpétuels.

Et quand tu n'es pas là
Je rêve que je dors
je rêve que je rêve.

VIII

My love for having given form to my desires
brought your lips to the sky of your words as a star
your kisses in the living night
and the wake of your arms around me
like a flame in the sign of conquest
my dreams are clear and perpetual
in this world.

And when you aren't here
I dream that I sleep
I dream that I dream.

IX

Où la vie se contemple tout est submerge
Monté les couronnes d'oubli
Les vertiges au cœur des metamorphoses
D'une écriture d'algues solaires
L'amour et l'amour.

Tes mains font le jour dans l'herbe
Tes yeux font l'amour en plein jour
Les sourires par la taille
Et tes lèvres par les ailes
Tu prends la place des caresses
Tu prends la place des réveils.

IX

When life contemplates itself everything is submerged
raising the crown of forgetfulness
the frenzy at the heart of the metamorphoses
of a writing of solar algae
love and love.

Your hands wake the day in the grass
your eyes make love in broad daylight
smiles by the waist
and your lips by the wings
you take the place of caresses
you take the place of awakenings.

X

Si calme la peau grise éteinte calcinée
Faible de la nuit prise dans ses fleurs de givre
Elle n'a plus de la lumière que les formes.

Amoureuse cela lui va bien d'être belle
Elle n'attend pas le printemps.

La fatigue la nuit le repos le silence
Tout un monde vivant entre des astres morts
La confiance dans la durée
Elle est toujours visible quand elle aime.

X

So calm the dull gray calcinated skin
frail from the night frozen in her flowers of frost
she has no more of the light than its forms.

Her love suits being pretty
she doesn't wait for spring.

Fatigue night repose silence
an entire living world between dead stars
confidence in the duration
She is always visible when she loves.

XI

Elle ne sait pas tendre des pièges
Elle a les yeux sur sa beauté
Si simple si simple séduire
Et ce sont ses yeux qui l'enchaînent
Et c'est sur moi qu'elle s'appuie
Et c'est sur elle qu'elle jette
Le filet volant des caresses.

XI

She doesn't know how to set traps
she has her eyes on her beauty
so simple so simple to seduce
and her eyes enchain
and she plies them on me
and she throws the flying net of caresses
over herself.

XII

Le mensonge menaçant les ruses dures et glissantes
Des bouches au fond des puits
        des yeux au fond des nuits
Et des vertus subites des filets à jeter au hazard
Les envies d'inventer d'admirables béquilles
Des faux des pièges entre les corps entre les lèvres
Des patiences massives des impatiences calculées
Tout ce qui s'impose et qui règne
Entre la liberté d'aimer
Et celle de ne pas aimer
Tout ce que tu ne connais pas.

XII

The lie menacing harsh and slippery ploys
from mouths in the depths of wells
from eyes in the depths of night
and sudden virtues nets thrown to chance
the desire to invent admirable crutches
falsehoods traps between bodies between lips
heavy patience calculated impatience
everything that imposes itself and reigns
between the freedom of loving
and that of not loving
everything that you don't know.

XIII

Amoureuse au secret derrière ton sourire
Toute nue les mots d'amour
Découvrent tes seins et ton cou
Et tes hanches et tes paupières
Découvrent toutes les caresses
Pour que les baisers dans tes yeux
Ne montrent que toi tout entière.

XIII

Woman in love
with the secret behind your smile
the words of love completely bare
uncover your breasts and your neck
your hips and eyelids
uncover every caress
so that the kisses in your eyes
reveal you alone
entirely.

XIV

Le sommeil a pris ton empreinte
Et la colore de tes yeux.

XIV

Sleep took your imprint
and the color of your eyes.

XV

Elle se penche sur moi
Le cœur ignorant
Pour voir si je l'aime
Elle a confiance elle oublie
Sous les nuages de ses paupières
Sa tête s'endort dans mes mains
Où sommes-nous
Ensemble inseparables
Vivants vivants
Vivant vivante
Et ma tête roule en ses rêves.

XV

She leans over me
the unknowing heart
to see if I love her
she is sure she forgets
under the clouds of her eyelids
her head falls asleep in my hands
where are we
together inseparable
living living
man and woman
my head rides in her dreams.

XVI

Bouches gourmandes des couleurs
Et les baisers qui les dessinent
Flamme feuille l'eau langoureuse
Une aile les tient dans sa paume
Un rire les renverse.

XVI

Mouths greedy for colors
and the kisses that outline them
flame leaf languorous water
a wing holds them in its palm
a laugh astounds them.

XVII

D'une seule caresse
Je te fais briller de tout ton éclat.

XVII

With a single caress
I make you shine in all of your brilliance.

XVIII

Bercée de chair frémissante pâture
Sur les rives du sang qui déchirent le jour
Le sang nocturne l'a chassée
Échevelée la gorge prise aux abus de l'orage
Victime abandonnée des ombres
Et des pas les plus doux et des désirs limpides
Son front ne sera plus le repos assuré
Ni ses yeux la faveur de rêver de sa voix
Ni ses mains les libératrices.

Criblée de feux criblée d'amour n'aimant personne
Elle se forge des douleurs démesurées
Et toutes ses raisons de souffrir disparaissent.

XVIII

Rocked by trembling flesh fodder
on the shores of blood that lacerate the day
the nocturnal blood chased
the disheveled throat caught in the storm's abuse
victim abandoned by the shadows
by the softest steps and limpid desires
her face will no longer be assured repose
nor her eyes the favor to dream of her voice
nor her hands liberators.

Sifted through fire through love loving no one
She forges herself through immeasurable suffering
and all her reasons for suffering disappear.

XIX

Une brise de danses
Par une route sans fin
Les pas des feuilles plus rapides
Tes nuages cachent ton ombre.

La bouche au feu d'hermine
A belles dents le feu
Caresse couleur de deluge
Tes yeux chassent la lumière.

La foudre rompt l'équilibre
Les fuseaux de la peur
Laissent tomber la nuit
Au fond de ton image.

XIX

Dancing breeze
on an endless road
the leaves' quickening pace
clouds hide your shadow.

Mouth of ermine fire
beautiful teeth
the fire caresses
the color of the flood
your eyes chase the light.

Lightning disrupts the equilibrium
the spindle legs of fear
allow night to fall
into the depths of your image.

XX

L'aube je t'aime j'ai toute la nuit dans les veines
Toute la nuit je t'ai regardée
J'ai tout à deviner je suis sûr des ténèbres
Elles me donnent le pouvoir
De t'envelopper
De t'agiter désir de vivre
Au sein de mon immobilité
Le pouvoir de te reveler
De te libérer de te perdre
Flamme invisible dans le jour.

Si tu t'en vas la porte s'ouvre sur le jour
Si tu t'en vas la porte s'ouvre sur moi-même.

XX

Dawn I love you I have the whole night in my veins
all night I watched you
I have everything to divine
I am sure of the darkness
giving me the power
to envelop you
to excite your desire for life
in the heart of my immobility
the power to reveal you
to liberate you to lose you
flame invisible by day.

If you go the door opens on the day
If you go the door opens on me.

XXI

Nos yeux se renvoient la lumière
Et la lumière le silence
A ne plus se reconnaître
A survivre à l'absence.

XXI

Our eyes return the light
and the light silence
no longer recognizing itself
surviving absence.

XXII

Le front aux vitres comme font les veilleurs
    de chagrin
Ciel dont j'ai dépassé la nuit
Plaines toutes petites dans mes mains ouvertes
Dans leur double horizon inerte indifferent
Le front aux vitres comme font les veilleurs
    de chagrin
Je te cherche par-delà l'attente
Par-delà moi-même
Et je ne sais plus tant je t'aime
Lequel de nous deux est absent.

XXII

Face against the panes like a sentinel of sorrow
sky through which I surpassed the night
plains so small in my open hands
in their indifferent inert double horizon
face against the panes like a sentinel of sorrow
I looked for you beyond waiting
beyond myself
and I love so much that I no longer know
which of us is absent.

XXIII

Voyage du silence
De mes mains à tes yeux

Et dans tes cheveux
Où des filles d'osier
S'adossent au soleil
Remuent les lèvres
Et laissent l'ombre à quatre feuilles
Gagner leur cœur chaud de sommeil.

XXIII

Voyage of silence
from my hands to your eyes

And in your hair
where willowy girls
recline on sunlight
move their lips
and let the four-leafed shadows
creep over their hearts warm with sleep.

XXIV

L'habituelle
Joue bonjour comme on joue l'aveugle
L'amour alors même qu'on y pense à peine
Elle est sur le rivage et dans tous les bras
Toujours
Les hasards sont à sa merci
Et les rêves des absents
Elle se sait vivante
Toutes les raisons de vivre.

XXIV

The habitual girl
fakes friendliness the way one fakes blindness
even the love that one scarcely considers
she is on the riverbank and in everyone's arms
always
the risks are at her mercy
and the dreams of those who are absent
she knows she is living
all the reasons for living.

XXV

Je me suis séparé de toi
Mais l'amour me précédait encore
Et quand j'ai tendu les bras
La douleur est venue s'y faire plus amère
Tout le désert à boire

Pour me séparer de moi-même.

XXV

I separated myself from you
but love preceded me once again
and when I held out my arms
pain came and made itself more bitter
an entire desert to drink

To separate me from myself.

XXVI

J'ai fermé les yeux pour ne plus rien voir
J'ai fermé les yeux pour pleurer
De ne plus te voir.

Où sont tes mains et les mains des caresses
Où sont tes yeux les quatre volontés du jour
Toi tout à perdre tu n'es plus là
Pour éblouir la mémoire des nuits.

Tout à perdre je me vois vivre.

XXVI

I closed my eyes so as not to see
I closed my eyes to cry
from no longer seeing you.

Where are your hands and the hands of caresses
where are your eyes the four whims of the day
with everything to lose you are no longer there
to dazzle the memory of the nights.

With everything to lose I see myself live.

XXVII

Les corbeaux battent la campagne
La nuit s'éteint
Pour une tête qui s'éveille
Les cheveux blancs le dernier rêve
Les mains se font jour de leur sang
De leurs caresses

Une étoile nommée azur
Et dont la forme est terrestre

Folle des cris à pleine gorge
Folle des rêves
Folle aux chapeaux de sœur cyclone
Enfance brève folle aux grands vents
Comment ferais-tu la belle la coquette

Ne rira plus
L'ignorance l'indifférence
Ne révèlent pas leur secret
Tu ne sais pas saluer à temps
Ni te comparer aux merveilles
Tu ne m'écoutes pas

Mais ta bouche partage l'amour
Et c'est par ta bouche
Et c'est derrière la buée de nos baisers
Que nous sommes ensemble.

XXVII

Ravens beat the countryside
night extinguished
for a waking head
the white hair the latest dream
hands bring blood to the light
of their caresses

A star named azure
of terrestrial form

Mad with full screams
mad with dreams
madness capped by her sister cyclone
brief childhood mad with powerful winds
How could you make beauty a coquette

Laugh no more
ignorance and indifference
don't reveal their secret
you don't know how to salute time
nor to compare yourself to marvels
you don't listen to me
but your mouth shares love
and it is with your mouth
and in the condensation of our kisses
that we are together.

XXVIII

Rouge amoureuse
Pour prendre part à ton plaisir
Je me colore de douleur.

J'ai vécu tu fermes les yeux
Tu t'enfermes en moi
Accepte donc de vivre.

Tout ce qui se répète est incomprehensible
Tu nais dans un miroir
Devant mon ancienne image.

XXVIII

Flushed woman in love
to take part in your pleasure
I color myself with pain.

I lived
you close your eyes
you enclose yourself in me
to accept life.

Everything that repeats itself is incomprehensible
you are born in a mirror
before my ancient image.

XXIX

Il fallait bien qu'un visage
Réponde à tous les noms du monde.

XXIX

It had to be important that a face
answer to all the names of the world.

Seconde nature

Second Nature

I

A genoux la jeunesse à genoux la colère
L'insulte saigne menace ruines
Les caprice n'ont plus leur couronne les fous
Vivent patiemment dans le pays de tous.

Le chemin de la mort dangereuse est barré
Par des funérailles superbes
L'épouvante est polie la misère a des charmes
Et l'amour prête à rire aux innocents obèses.

Agréments naturels éléments en musique
Virginités de boue artifices de singe
Respectable fatigue honorable laideur
Travaux délicieux où l'oubli se repaît.
La souffrance est là par hazard
Et nous sommes le sol sur quoi tout est bâti
Et nous sommes partout
Où se lève le ciel des autres

Partout où le refus de vivre est inutile.

I

Youth on its knees anger on its knees
the insult bleeds threatens ruins
whims no longer have their crown the mad
live patiently in our world.

The road of dangerous death is blocked
by superb funeral processions
dread is polite misery has its charms
and love is ready to laugh at the obese innocents.

Natural pleasures musical elements
virginities of filth ape artifices
respectable fatigue honorable ugliness
delicious work where oblivion gorges itself.
Suffering is present by chance
and we are the ground on which everything is built
and we are everywhere
where the others' heaven rises

Everywhere that the refusal of life is futile.

II

Tout les larmes sans raison
Toute la nuit dans ton miroir
La vie du plancher au plafond
Tu doutes de la terre et de ta tête
Dehors tout est mortel
Pourtant tout est dehors
Tu vivras de la vie d'ici
Et de l'espace misérable
Qui répond à tes gestes
Qui placarde tes mots
Sur un mur incomprehensible

Et qui donc pense à ton visage?

II

All the senseless tears
all night in your mirror
life from floor to ceiling
earth and mind cause your doubts
outside everything is mortal
and everything is outside
you will live this life from here
and from this miserable space
that responds to your gestures
that posts your words
on an incomprehensible wall

and who therefore thinks of your face?

III

La solitude l'absence
Et ses coups de lumière
Et ses balances
N'avoir rien vu rien compris

La solitude le silence
Plus émouvant
Au crépuscule de la peur
Que le premier contact des larmes

L'ignorance l'innocence
La plus cachée
La plus vivante
Qui met la mort au monde.

III

Solitude absence
flashes of light
and balances
having seen nothing understood nothing

Solitude silence
more moving
at the twilight of fear
than at the beginning of tears

Ignorance innocence
the most hidden
the most living
brings death into the world.

IV

A droite je regarde dans les plus beaux yeux
A gauche entre les ailes aveugles de la peur
A droite à jour avec moi-même
A gauche sans raison aux sources de la vie.

J'écoute tous les mots que j'ai su inspirer
Et qui ne sont plus à personne
Je partage l'amour qui ne me connaît pas
Et j'oublie le besoin d'aimer.

Mais je tourne la tête pour reprendre corps
Pour nourrir le souci mortel d'être vivant
La honte sur un fond de grimaces natales.

IV

To the right I look into the most beautiful eyes
to the left between wings blind with fear
to the right caught up with myself
to the left senselessly at the springs of life.

I listen to all the words that I knew how to inspire
and that no longer belong to anyone
I share the love that doesn't know me
and I forget the need to love.

But I turn my head to regain body
to nourish the mortal concern of being alive
the shame on a bed of natal grimaces.

V

En l'honneur des muets des aveugles des sourds
A la grande pierre noire sur les épaules
Les disparitions du monde sans mystère.

Mais aussi pour les autres à l'appel des choses
      par leur nom
La brûlure de toutes les métamorphoses
La chaîne entière des aurores dans la tête
Tous les cris qui s'acharnent à briser les mots

Et qui creusent la bouche et qui creusent les yeux
Où les couleurs furieuses défont les brumes de l'attente
Dressent l'amour contre la vie les morts en rêvent
Les bas-vivants partagent les autres sont esclaves
De l'amour comme on peut l'être de la liberté.

V

In honor of the dumb the blind the deaf
the great black stone on their shoulders
the disappearance of the world without mystery.

But also for the others calling things by their name
the burn of all metamorphosis
the entire chain of dawns in the head
all the screams bent on shattering words

which empty the mouth and empty the eyes
where furious colors dispel the mists of waiting
set love against the life the dead dream of
the lowly share the others are slaves
of love as one can be a slave of freedom.

VI

La vie est accrochée aux armes menaçantes
Et c'est elle qui tue tout ce qui l'a comprise
Montre ton sang mère des miroirs
Ressemblance montre ton sang
Que les sources des jours simples se dessèchent
De honte comme des crépuscules.

VI

Life is caught in menacing arms
and life kills everything that understands it
mother of mirrors show your blood
resemblance show your blood
the source of simple days dries up
from shame as from twilight.

VII

L'ignorance à chanter la nuit
Où le rire perd ses couleurs
Où les déments qui le dévorent
S'enivrent d'une goutte de sang
Rayonnante dans des glaciers.

Les grands passages de la chair
Entre les os et les fatigues
Au front la mort à petit feu
Et les vitres vides d'alcool.
Frémissent comme l'oiseau de tête.

Le silence a dans la poitrine
Tous les flambeaux éteints du cœur.
Parmi les astres de mémoire
Les plaines traînent des orages
Et les baisers se multiplient

Dans les grands réflecteurs des rêves.

VII

Not knowing how to sing the night
wherein laughter loses its colors
wherein the mad who devour this laughter
grow drunk from a drop of blood
radiant in ice.

The great passages of the flesh
between bones and fatigues
at the forefront slow death
and the windows empty of alcohol.
Trembling like the lead bird.

Silence has in its breast
all the heart's extinguished flames.
Among the starbursts of memory
the plains extend storms
and kisses multiply.

In the grand reflectors of dreams.

VIII

Les ombres blanches
Les fronts crevés des impuissances
Devant des natures idiots
Des grimaces de murs
Le langage du rire
Et pour sauver la face
Les prisonniers de neige fondent dans leur prison
La face où les reflets des murs
Creusent l'habitude de la mort

VIII

White shadows
faces pitted with weakness
before dumb nature
the grimace of walls
the language of laughter
and to save face
the prisoners of snow melt in their prison
the face in which the wall's reflections
hollow the habit of death.

IX

Les yeux brûlés du bois
Le masque inconnu papillon d'aventure
Dans les prisons absurdes
Les diamants du cœur
Collier du crime.

Des menaces montrent les dents
Mordent le rire
Arrachent les plumes du vent
Les feuilles mortes de la fuite.

La faim couverte d'immondices
Étreint le fantôme du blé
La peur en loques perce les murs
Des plaines pâles miment le froid.

Seule la douleur prend feu.

IX

Eyes burning with wood
unknown mask butterfly of adventure
in absurd prisons
diamonds of the heart
necklace of crime.

Dangers show their teeth
tear into laughter
pluck plumes from the wind
dead leaves from flight.

Hunger covered in filth
grips the phantom wheat
fear in rags pierces the walls
pale plains mime the cold.

Only pain catches fire.

X

Les oiseaux maintenant volent de leurs propres ombres
Les regards n'ont pas ce pouvoir
Et les découvertes ont beau jeu
L'œil fermé brûlé dans toutes les têtes
L'homme est entre les images
Entre les hommes
Tous les hommes entre les hommes.

X

Now birds fly from their own shadows
eyes lack this power
and the discoveries played well
a closed eye burns in any head
man is between the images
between men
every man between men.

XI

Aux grandes inondations de soleil
Qui décolorent les parfums
Aux confins des saisons magiques
Aux soleils renversés
Beaux comme des gouttes d'eau
Les désirs se dédoublent
Voici qu'ils ont choisi
Les tortures les plus contraires
Visage admirable tout nu
Ridicule refusé comme rebelle
Dépaysé
Tournure secrete
Chemins de chair et ciel de tête
Et toi complice miserable
Avec des larmes entre les feuilles
Et ce grand mur que tu defends
Pour rien
Parce que tu croiras toujours
Avoir fait le mal par amour
Ce grand mur que tu defends
Inutilement.

Sous les paupières dans les chevelures
Je berce celles qui pensent à moi
Elles ont changé d'attitude
Depuis les temps vulgaires
Elles ont leur part de refus sur les bras
Les caresses n'ont pas délivré leur poitrine
Leurs gestes je les règle en leur disant adieu
Le souvenir de mes paroles exige le silence
Comme l'audace engage toute la dignité.

XI

To the great floods of sunlight
that discolor perfumes
to the frontiers of magical seasons
to inverted suns
beautiful as drops of water
desires divide themselves
they have chosen
the most adverse tortures
admirable face entirely bare
ridicule rejected as rebellion
disoriented
a secret course
flesh roads, heaven head
and you, miserable accomplice
with tears between the leaves
and this great wall that you defend
for nothing
because you will always believe
you've done wrong through your love
this great wall that you defend
uselessly.

Beneath eyelids in hair
I cradle those who think of me
they have changed their minds
since vulgar times
having had their share of rejections in their arms
caresses haven't freed their chest
I measure their gestures when saying goodbye
the memory of my words demands silence
the way audacity enlists dignity.

Entendez-moi
Je parle pour les quelques hommes qui se taisent
Les meilleurs.

Hear me
I speak for those men who quiet themselves
the best.

XII

Sonnant les cloches du hasard à toute volée
Ils jouèrent à jeter les cartes par la fenêtre
Les désirs du gagnant prirent corps d'horizon
Dans le sillage des délivrances.

Il brûla les racines les sommets disparurent
Il brisa les barrières du soleil des étangs
Dans les plaines nocturnes le feu chercha l'aurore
Il commença tous les voyages par la fin
Et sur toutes les routes

Et la terre devint à se perdre nouvelle.

XII

Tolling bells of chance with each flight
they played at throwing the cards through the window
the desire to win took the body of the horizon
in the wake of deliverances.

He burned the roots the summits disappeared
he broke the boundaries of the sun from pools
in nocturnal plains the fire looked for the dawn
He began every voyage at the end
and on every road.

And the earth came to lose itself anew.

XIII

Pour voir se reproduire le soupçon des tombeaux
On ne s'embrasse plus la souffrance s'anime
Poitrine comme un incendie bien isolé vaincu
Le feu ne connaît plus son semblable qui dort
Il prend les ciseaux des jours et des nuits par la main
Il descend sur les branches les plus basses
Il tombe il a sur terre les débris d'une ombre.

XIII

To see the suspicion of graves reproduce
we no longer embrace the suffering comes alive
chest like an isolated fire beaten
this fire no longer knows its equal who sleeps
taking the scissors of days and nights by the hand
descending to the lowest branches
falling to the ground the remains of a shadow.

XIV

Le piège obscur des hontes
Avec entre les doigts les brûlures du jour

Aussi loin que l'amour

Mais tout est semblable
Sur la peau d'abondance.

XIV

The obscure trap of shame
the remains of the day between its fingers

as far as love

but everything is the same
on the skin of abundance.

XV

Danseur faible qui dans les coins
Avance sa poitrine étroite
Il perd haleine il est dans un terrier
La nuit lui lèche les vertebras
La terre mord son destin
Je suis sur le toit
Tu n'y viendras plus.

XV

Weak dancer in the corners
advances his narrow chest
loses breath in a hole
night licks his vertebrae
the earth bites into his destiny
I am on the roof
you will no longer come here.

XVI

Ni crime de plomb
Ni justice de plume
Ni vivante d'amour
Ni mort de désir.

Elle est tranquille indifférente
Elle est fière d'être facile
Les grimaces sont dans les yeux
Des autres ceux qui la remuent.

Elle ne peut pas être seule
Elle se couronne d'oubli
Et sa beauté couvre les heures
Qu'il faut pour n'être plus personne.
Elle va partout fredonnant
Chanson monotone inutile
La forme de son visage.

XVI

Neither leaden crime
nor the justice of the pen
neither living on love
nor dying of desire.

She is tranquil indifferent
she is proud of being easy
Grimaces are in the eyes
of those that move her.

She is unable to be alone
she crowns herself with oblivion
and her beauty fills the hours
required to no longer be someone.
She goes everywhere humming
useless monotone songs
The form of her face.

XVII

Dignité symétrique vie bien partagée
Entre la vieillesse des rues
Et la jeunesse des nuages
Volets fermés les mains tremblantes de claret
Les mains comme des fontaines
Et la tête domptée.

XVII

Symmetrical dignity life well shared
between the age of the roads
and the youth of the clouds
closed shutters hands trembling in clarity
hands like fountains
and the subdued mind.

XVIII

Tristesse aux flots de pierre.

Des lames poignardent des lames
Des vitres cassent des vitres
Des lampes éteignent des lampes

Tant de liens brisés.

La flèche et la blessure
L'œil et la lumière
L'ascension et la tête.

Invisible dans le silence.

XVIII

Sadness in waves of rock.

Razors stab razors
Windows break windows
Lamps extinguish lamps

So many broken links.

The arrow and the wound
Eye and light
Ascension and mind.

Invisible in the silence.

XIX

Les prisonniers ont envie de rire
Ils ont perdu les clefs de la curiosité
Ils chargent le désir de vivre
De chaînes légères
D'anciens reproches les réjouissent encore
La paresse n'est plus un mystère
L'indépendance est en prison.

XIX

Prisoners want to laugh
they have lost the key to curiosity
they burden their desire to live
with light chains
still delighting in ancient disgraces
laziness is no longer a mystery
independence is in prison.

XX

Ils n'animent plus la lumière
Ils ne jouent plus avec le feu
Pendus au mépris des victories
Et limitant tous leurs semblables
Criant l'orage à bras ouverts
Aveugles d'avoir sur la face
Tous les yeux comme des baisers
La face battue par les larmes
Ils ont capturé la peur et l'ennui
Les solitaires pour tous
Ont réduit le silence
Et lui font faire des grimaces
Dans le désert de leur présence.

XX

They no longer animate the light
they no longer play with fire
caught in contempt of victories
and limiting their equals
decrying the storm with open arms
blind for having on a face
all eyes like kisses
face beaten by tears
they have captured fear and boredom
for all of us these solitary figures
have lessened silence
and made it grimace
in the desert of their presence.

XXI

Le tranquille fléau doublé de plaints
Tourbillonne sur des nuques gelées
Autant de fleurs à patins
De baisers de buée
Pour ce jet d'eau que les fièvres
Couronnent du feu des larmes
L'agonie du plus haut désir
Nouez les rires aux douleurs
Nouez les pillards aux vivants
Supplices misérables
Et la chute contre le vertige.

XXI

Tranquil scourge doubled with complaint
whirls on the frozen napes
so many flowers
steamy kisses
for this gush of water that fevers
crowned by fire of tears
the agony of the highest desire
twists laughter into pain
twists the pillagers to the living
miserable tortures
and the fall against frenzy.

XXII

Le soleil en éveil sur la face crispée
De la mer barre toute et toute bleue
Sur un homme au grand jour sur l'eau qui se dérobe
Des nuées d'astres mûrs leur sens et leur durée
Soulèvent ses paupières à bout de vivre exténuées.

D'immortelles misères pour violer l'ennui
Installent le repos sur un roc de fatigues
Le corps creux s'est tourné l'horizon s'est noué
Quelles lumières où les conduire le regard levé
Le front têtu bondit sur l'eau comme une pierre
Sur une voie troublée de sources de douleur

Et des rides toujours nouvelles le purifient.

XXII

The sun rising on the shriveled face
of the entirely barred and blue sea
on a man in broad daylight on the water that escapes
swarms of stars ripening their meaning and duration
raising his eyelids at the end of an enfeebled life.

From immortal miseries to rape boredom
installing repose on a rock of fatigue
the empty bodies turn themselves the horizon ties itself
the lights to which the risen gaze drives them
the stubborn face bounces across the water like a stone
on a path troubled by springs of pain

And ever new wrinkles purify it.

Comme une image

Like an Image

I

Je cache les sombres trésors
Des retraites inconnues
Le cœur des forêts le sommeil
D'une fusée ardente
L'horizon nocturne
Qui me couronne
Je vais la tête la première
Saluant d'un secret nouveau
La naissance des images.

I

I conceal the dark treasures
of unknown recesses
the heart of the forests the sleep
of a burning flare
the nocturnal horizon
that crowns me
I advance head first
greeting with a new secret
the birth of images.

II

La présence de la lavande au chevet des maladies
Son damier les races prudentes desséchées
Pour changer les jours de fête leur serrer le cœur
La main de tous les diables sur les draps.

Supplice compliqué la branche aux singes
            aux calembours
L'amitié la moitié la mère et la bannière
On tend la perche à la défaite
Les vieux sages ont leurs nerfs des grands jours.

Des lampes éteintes des lampes de betel
Apparaissent au tournant d'un front
Puis la plante des têtes en série
Jumelles fil-à-fil et le sang bien coiffé

Soumises à la croissance.

II

The presence of lavender at the bedside of the sick
checkerboard withered prudent races
clenching their heart to change the holidays
the hand of every devil on the sheets.

Complicated torture monkey pun's branch
friendship half mother banner
one extends the pole to defeat
the old sages have nerves for glory.

Extinguished lamps betel lamps
appear with the turning of a face
then the plant of heads in a series
twins thread by thread and well-dressed blood

Submissive to faith.

III

Bouquet des sèves le brasier que chevauche le vent
Fumées en tête les armées de la prise du monde
L'écume des tourments aériens la presence
Les attaches du front le plus haut de la terre.

III

Sap bouquet furnace astride the wind
armies who have taken the world smoking
the foam of celestial torments presence
the bonds of the front the highest on the earth.

IV

Armure de proie le parfum noir rayonne
Les arbres sont coiffés d'un paysage en amande
Berceau de tous les paysages les clés les dés
Les plaines de soucis les montagnes d'albâtre
Les lampes de banlieue la pudeur les orages
Les gestes imprévus voués au feu
Les route qui séparent la mer de ses noyés
Tous les rébus indéchiffrables.

La fleur de chardon construit un château
Elle monte aux échelles du vent
Et des graines à tête de mort.
Des étoiles d'ébène sur les vitres luisantes
Promettent tout à leurs amants
Les autres qui simulent
Maintiennent l'ordre de plomb.

Muet malheur de l'homme
Son visage petit matin
S'ouvre comme une prison
Ses yeux sont des têtes coupées
Ses doigts lui servent à compter

A mesurer à prendre à convaincre
Ses doigts savent le ligoter.

IV

Armor of prey black perfume radiates
trees are trimmed from a landscape in almond
cradle of all landscapes keys dice
marigold plains alabaster mountains
suburban lamps prudence storms
unexpected gestures sworn to the fire
the routes that separate the sea from its dead
all the indecipherable riddles.

The thistle flower builds a castle
it climbs the ladder of the wind
and seeds momento mori.
Ebony stars on glistening windows
promise everything to their lovers
the others who fake it
maintain the leaden order.

The silent unhappiness of the man
his face early morning
opens like a prison
his eyes are severed heads
his fingers serve to count

to measure to take to convince
his fingers know how to bind him.

Ruine du public
Son émotion est en morceaux
Son enthousiasme à l'eau
Les parures suspendues aux terreurs de la foudre
Pâturages livides où des rochers bondissent
Pour en finir
Une tombe ornée de très jolis bibelots
Un voile de soie sur les lenteurs de la luxure
Pour en finir
Une hache dans le dos d'un seul coup.

Dans les ravins du sommeil
Le silence dresse ses enfants
Voici le bruit fatal qui crève les tympans
La poussiéreuse mort des couleurs
L'idiotie
Voici le premier paresseux
Et les mouvements machinaux de l'insomnie
L'oreille les roseaux à courber comme un casque
L'oreille exigeante l'ennemie oubliée dans la brume
Et l'inépuisable silence
Qui bouleverse la nature en ne la nommant pas
Qui tend des pièges souriants
Ou des absences à faire peur
Brise tous les miroirs des lèvres.

En pleine mer dans des délicats
Aux beaux jours les vagues à toutes voiles
Et le sang mène à tout
C'est une place sans statue

Public ruin
its emotion in pieces
its enthusiasm at sea
finery suspended by the terrors of the lightning
livid pastures where rocks bounce
to an end
a tomb decorated by three pretty trinkets
a veil of silk over the slowness of lust
to an end
an axe in the back with a single blow.

In the ravines of sleep
silence addresses its infants
here the fatal noise that splits the eardrum
the dusty death of colors
idiocy
here the first laziness
and the mechanical motions of insomnia
the ear the reeds bow like a helmet
the demanding ear a forgotten enemy in the fog
and the inexhaustible silence
that upsets nature in not naming it
that spreads smiling snares
or absences that frighten
shatter all the mirrors of the lips.

At sea in delicate arms
happy days waves at full sail
and the blood leads to everything
A place without a statue

Sans rumeurs sans pavillon noir
Une place nue irisée
Où toutes les fleurs errantes
Les fleurs au gré de la lumière
Ont caché de féeries d'audace
C'est un bijou d'indifférence
A la mesure de tous les cœurs
Un bijou ciselé de rires
C'est une maison mystérieuse
Où des enfants déjouent les hommes.

Aux alentours de l'espoir
En pure perte
Le calme fait le vide.

Without rumors without black pavilions
an iridescent nude place
where all the wandering flowers
flowers at the will of the light
have hidden audacious fairies
A jewel of indifference
equal to all hearts
a chiseled jewel of laughter
A mysterious house
where children baffle adults.

In the periphery of hope
in pure loss
calm creates a void.

V

Porte comprise
Porte facile
Une captive
Ou personne.
Des torrents décousus
Et des vaisseaux de sable
Qui font tomber les feuilles.

La lumière et la solitude.

Ici pour nous ouvrir les yeux
Seules les cendres bougent.

V

Door included
a simple door
a captive
or person.
Unsuited by floods
and vessels of sand
that make the leaves fall.

Light and solitude.

Here
to open our eyes
only ashes stir.

VI

Le hibou le corbeau le vautour
Je ne crois pas aux autres oiseaux
La plus lourde route s'est pendue
Toutes les tours à paysage au jeu des astres
Les ombres mal placées ravagées émiettées
Les arbres du soleil ont une écorce de fumée.

La vitre mue. Ma force me cahote
Me fait trébucher. Au loin des pièges de bétail
Et l'aimant des allées la ruse pour les éviter.

Bien entendu les enfants sont complices
Mains masquées les enfants éteignent les crêtes et
        les plumes

Candeur aux neuf rires de proie
L'opaque tremblement des ciseaux qui font peur
La nuit n'a jamais rien vu la nuit prend l'air.

Tous les baisers trouvaient la rive.

VI

Owl raven vulture
I don't believe in other birds
the heaviest route hung itself
all the towers against the landscape in the play of the stars
poorly arranged shadows ravaged crumbled
the trees of the sunlight have a bark of smoke.

The window molts. My strength jolts
makes me stumble. Far from animal traps
and the lover of the lanes plays a trick to avoid them.

Of course the children are accessories
hands masked the children extinguish the crests
        and plumes

New candor the laughter of prey
the opaque trembling of fearsome scissors
night has never seen anything the night gasps.

Every kiss would find the river bank.

VII

Où mettez-vous le bec seul
Vos ailes qu'éveillent-elles seul
Des boules de mains le pouvoir absolu seul
Et le prestige des rapaces par-dessus seul
Ruines des ronces seul
L'œuf des mains enchantées inépuisables seul
Que les doigts fassent le signe du zéro seul
Les lambris des cascades l'eau tend la main seul
Au loin la neige et ses sanglots seul
La nuit fanée la terre absente seul.

VII

Where do you put the beak alone
Your wings that wake alone
balls from hands absolute power alone
and the prestige of birds of prey hovering alone
brambles in ruin alone
the egg of the enchanted inexhaustible hands alone
that the fingers might make the sign of zero alone
the canopy of cascades water extends a hand alone
from afar snow and sobs alone
the faded night the absent earth alone.

VIII

Vous êtes chez moi. Suis-je chez moi?
J'ai toute la place nécessaire
Pour qu'il n'y ait pas de spectacle
Chez moi.
Ailleurs la chaîne—les anneaux respirent—
Des dormeurs
Les arcs tendus de leurs poitrines
Au défi des chemins
Au hazard l'on entend frapper au hazard ou crier
        sans raison
Les ponts respirent
Et les baisers sont à l'image des reflets.

Au fond de la lumière
A la surface de leur lumière
Les yeux se ferment
Les berceaux—les paupières—des couleurs obscures
Les cloches de paille des étincelles
Le sable tire sa révérence
Aux cachettes des oasis
Sans univers à ses pieds nus
L'oubli—le ciel—se met tout nu.

Les étoiles ont pris la place de la nuit
Il n'y a plus que des étoiles toutes les aubes
Et la naissance de toutes les saisons du sommeil
Le visage des mains inconnues qui se lient
Vies échangées toutes les découvertes
Pour animer les formes confondues
Claires ou closes lourdes ou toutes en tête
Pour dormir ou pour s'éveiller
Le front contre les étoiles.

VIII

You are at my house. Am I at home?
I have all the necessary room
for there not to be a spectacle
at my house.
Elsewhere the chain—the links breathe—
sleepers
their chests spread
against the road
by chance one hears knocking by chance or screams
    without reason
the bridges breathe
and the kisses belong to the image of reflections.

In the depth of the light
on the surface of their light
eyes close
the cradles—eyelids—of obscure colors
the bells of hay of sparks
the sand removes its reverence
to the hiding of an oasis
without the universe at its naked feet
oblivion—the sky—strips itself bare.

Stars have taken the place of the night
there is nothing more than the stars every dawn
and the birth of all the seasons of sleep
the faces of unknown hands link themselves
lives exchanged every discovery
to animate the confused forms
clear or closed weighty or entirely in the mind
to sleep or wake
face against the stars.

IX

Révolte de la neige
Qui succombe bientôt frappée d'un seul coup d'ombre
Juste le temps de rapprocher l'oubli des morts
De faire pâlir la terre.

Aux marches des torrents
Des filles de cristal aux tempes fraîches
Petites qui fleurissent et faibles qui sourient
Pour faire la part de l'eau séduisent la lumière

Des chutes de soleil des aurores liquids

Et quand leurs baisers deviennent invisibles
Elles vont dormir dans la gueule des lions.

IX

Revolt of the snow
that succumbs soon struck by a single shadow
Time alone to reproach the oblivion of the dead
to bleach the earth.

In the steps of the flood
crystal girls with fresh temples
little ones who flower and weak ones who smile
to play the part of the water seducing the light

Falling suns liquid dawns

And when their kisses become invisible
they go to sleep in the mouths of lions.

X

Mange ta faim entre dans cet œuf
Où le plâtre s'abat
Où l'arôme du sommeil
Paralyse l'ivresse
Des bêtes en avance
Des bêtes matinales aux ailes transparentes
Se pavanent sur l'eau
Le loup-corail séduit l'épine-chevalière
Toutes les chevelures des îles
Recouvrent des grappes d'oiseaux
La fraise-rossignol chante son sang qui fume
Et les mouches éblouissantes
Rêvent d'une aube criblée d'étoiles
De glaçons et de coquillages.

Lourd le ciel coule à pic
Le ciel des morts sans reflets.

X

Eat your hunger enters this egg
where the plaster crashes down
where the aroma of sleep
paralyzes drunkenness
beasts out front
morning beasts with transparent wings
strut on water
the coral wolf seduces the thorn knight
all the islands' hair
recover the clusters of birds
the strawberry nightingale sings its smoking blood
and the dazzling bugs
dream of a dawn coursed with stars
with blocks of ice and shells.

Heavy the sky flows pointedly
the sky of the dead without reflection.

XI

Reflets racines dans l'eau calme
Des collines cavaliers
Sous leur robe
L'infortune parle à son maître
Le sourd a des rages de troupeau
Comme un fagot de fouets
Veille des décors résignés
Les oiseaux sortent de la nuit
Avec des chansons de secours
Un coq de panique jaillit
Des vignes de l'orage
Les vendanges sont faites
Sur son pupitre le front s'étale
comme le froid sur le miroir des morts
Entre deux semblables
Le lourd naufrage du sommeil.

XI

Reflections roots in calm water
cavalier hills
under their dress
the unfortunate speaks to its master
the deaf one has the mania of the herd
like a bundle of whips
on the eve of resigned decorations
the birds leave the night
with songs of aid
a panic cock gushes
from the vines of the storm
the grapes are harvested
on its stand the face reveals itself
like the cold on the mirror of the dead
between two equals
the heavy shipwreck of sleep.

XII

Passage où la vue détourne d'un coup la pensée
Une ombre s'agrandit cherche son univers
Et tombe horizontalement
Dans le sens de la marche

La verdure caresse les épaules de la rue
Le soir verse du feu dans de verres de couleur
Comme à la fête
Un éventail d'alcool.

Suspendue par la bouche aux délires livides
Une tête délicieuse et ses vœux ses conquêtes
Une bouche éclatante
Obstinée et toujours à son premier baiser.

Passage où la vie est visible.

XII

Passage where the view instantly turns thought
a shadow expands looking for its universe
and falls horizontally
into the procession

The greenery caresses the shoulders of the street
night pours fire in colored glasses
as at the party
a range of alcohol.

Suspended by the mouth in livid deliriums
a delightful head and its vows and conquests
a dazzling mouth
obstinate and always on its first kiss.

Passage where life is visible.

XIII

Je sors des caves de l'angoisse
Des courbes lentes de la peur
Je tombe dans un puits de plumes
Pavots je vous retrouve
Sans y songer
Dans un miroir fermé
Vous êtes aussi beaux que des fruits
Et si lourds ô mes maîtres
Qu'il vous faut des ailes pour vivre
Ou mes rêves.

L'enfance reste chez elle
A rougir de ses devoirs
A mériter la vie
Avec ses jeux de toutes les couleurs
Ses cahiers tondus ses plumiers acides
Une main se ferme se pose
Les mains de l'enfant
Comme des grenouilles.

Mais voici que s'abat se dresse se dandine
La poussière arrogante
Sans carcasse toute de charmes
La toute pelée la curieuse
Un palais la salue la reçoit l'accompagne
Avec sa façade avec le grand livre d'origine
Avec les clefs qui sont une offense aux murailles

XIII

I leave the cellars of anguish
the slow sweep of fear
I fall in a well of feathers
I recover poppies
without dreaming of you
in a closed mirror
you are as beautiful as fruit
and so heavy O my masters
you need wings to live
or my dreams.

Youth stays with her
blushing at responsibilities
deserving life
with games in every color
cut notebooks acid pens
a hand closes poses
the child's hands
like frogs.

But here what tumbles down stands up waddles
arrogant dust
every charm bodiless
the curious one entirely peeled
a palace greets her receives her accompanies her
with her face with the great book of origins
with keys that are an offense to the walls

Les rideaux soulevés du sourire
A croire aussi que le triple dedans
N'est pas mesuré par les rides.

La plus petite course du lézard
Dément toutes les precautions
La plus petite mort du bois
Quand la hache casse le fil
Et délivre un oiseau
Le coup d'ailes de la surprise.

L'armature des rousses éclatante parure
Et ce mépris pour toutes les plantes souterraines
Pour bénir les poisons pour honorer les fièvres
Les sources sont couronnées d'ombre
Le corps partage ses conquêtes
Mais sa jeunesse est au secret.

Pavots renoncez-vous
Au dur trajet des graines.

The curtains raised with a smile
to believe that the triple inside
is not measured by the folds.

The shortest course of the lizard
refutes all precautions
the least dead wood
when the axe breaks the thread
and frees a bird
the wingbeat of surprise.

The armature of the redhead's dazzling attire
and this contempt for all the underground plants
to bless poisons and honor fevers
springs are crowned with shadows
the body shares its conquests
but its youth is secret.

Poppies renounce yourselves
in the hard trajectory of grains.

XIV

A l'assaut des jardins
Les saisons sont partout à la fois
Passion de l'été pour l'hiver
Et la tendresse des deux autres
Les souvenirs comme des plumes
Les arbres ont brisé le ciel
Un beau chêne gâché de brume
La vie des oiseaux ou la vie des plumes
Et tout un panache frivole
Avec de souriantes craintes
Et la solitude bavarde.

XIV

With the assault of gardens
seasons are everywhere at once
the passion of the summer for the winter
and the tenderness of the two others
memories like feathers
the trees crack the sky
a beautiful oak tree spoiled by fog
the life of birds or the life of feathers
and an entire frivolous panache
with smiling fears
and babbling solitude.

Défense de savoir
I

Knowledge Forbidden
I

I

Ma présence n'est pas ici
Je suis habillé de moi-même
Il n'y a pas de planète qui tienne
La clarté existe sans moi.

Née de ma main sur mes yeux
Et me détournant de ma voie
L'ombre m'empêche de marcher
Sur ma couronne d'univers
Dans le grand miroir habitable
Miroir brisé mouvant inverse
Où l'habitude et la surprise
Créent l'ennui à tour de rôle.

I

My presence is not here
I'm dressed in myself
no planet holds together
clarity exists without me.

Born with my hand over my eyes
and turning me from my way
shadows prevent me from walking
on my crown the universe
in the great inhabitable mirror
broken mirror turning around
where habit and surprise
create boredom by turns.

II

L'aventure est pendue au cou de son rival
L'amour dont le regard se retrouve ou s'égare
Sur les places des yeux désertes ou peuplées.

Toutes les aventures de la face humaine
Cris sans échos signes de morts temps hors mémoire
Tant de beaux visages si beaux
Que les larmes les cachent
Tant d'yeux aussi sûrs de leur nuit
Que des amants mourant ensemble
Tant de baisers sous roche et tant d'eau sans nuages
Apparitions surgies d'absences éternelles
Tout était digne d'être aimé
Les trésors sont des murs et leur ombre est aveugle
Et l'amour est au monde pour l'oubli du monde.

II

Adventure is hung around the neck of its rival
love whose gaze finds or loses itself
in place of deserted or populated eyes.

All the adventures of the human face
cries without echoes signs of the dead time outside
     memory
so many beautiful faces so beautiful
that tears hide themselves
so many eyes as sure of their night
as lovers dying together
so many kisses under rock and so much water
     without clouds
apparitions spill from eternal absences
everything was worthy of love
treasures are walls and their shadows are blind
and love is in the world so that the world
     may forget.

III

Accrochés aux désirs de vitesse
Et cernant de plomb les plus lents
Les murs ne se font plus face
Des êtres multiples des éventails d'êtres
Des êtres-chevelures
Dorment dans un reflet sanglant
Dans sa rage fauve
La terre montre ses paumes.

Les yeux se sont fermés
Parce que le front brûle
Courage nocturne diminuer l'ombre
De moitié miroir de l'ombre
Moitié du monde la tête tombe
Entre le sommeil et le rêve.

III

Caught by a desire for speed
and surrounded by the slowest bullets
walls no longer stand up
multiple beings fan shaped beings
living hair
asleep in a bleeding reflection
in a wild rage
earth shows its palms.

Its eyes are closed
because its forehead is burning
nocturnal courage shrinks the shadow
from half the mirror of the shadow
half the world the head falls
between sleep and dream.

IV

Il fait toujours nuit quand je dors
Nuit supposée imaginaire
Qui ternit au réveil toutes les transparences
La nuit use la vie mes yeux que je deliver
N'ont jamais rien trouvé à leur puissance.

IV

It is always night when I sleep
night presumed imaginary
that tarnishes every transparency on waking
night exhausts life eyes that I liberate
have never found anything in their power.

V

Les hommes errants plus forts que les nains habituels
Ne se rencontrent pas. L'on raconte
Qu'ils se dévoreraient. La force de la force
Carcasses de connaissances carcasses d'ânes
Toujours rôdant dans les cerveaux et dans les chairs
Vous êtes bien téméraires dans vos suppositions.

Savante dégradation des blancs
Au ventre à table tout le matériel nécessaire
L'espoir sur tous les yeux met ses verres taillés
Le cœur on s'aperçoit que malgré tout l'on vit
Tandis qu'aux plages nues un seul homme inusable
Confond toute couleur avec la ligne droite
Mêle toute pensée à l'immobilité
Insensible de sa présence éternelle
Et fait le tour du monde et fait le tour du temps
La tête prisonnière dans son corps lié.

V

Stronger than the typical dwarf wandering men
don't encounter each other. Someone says
they would devour each other. The power of power
acquaintances' corpses donkeys' corpses
forever prowling in the brain and in the flesh
you are very reckless in your suppositions.

The knowing degradation of whites
stomach to table is all that's required
hope puts its cut glasses over every eye
we notice our hearts despite our lives
while on nude beaches one man alone durable
confuses every color with the straight line
mixes every thought with immobility
insensitive to his eternal presence
and tours the world and time
the mind imprisoned in its affiliated body.

VI

La nuit les yeux les plus confiants nient
Jusqu'à l'épuisement
La nuit sans une paille
Le regard fixe dans une solitude d'encre.

VI

The night the most confident eyes deny
to the point of exhaustion
the gaze freezes the flawless night
in a solitude of ink.

VII

Quel beau spectacle mais quel beau spectacle
A proscrire. Sa visibilité parfaite
Me rendrait aveugle.

Des chrysalides de mes yeux
Naîtra mon sosie ténébreux
Parlant à contre-jour soupçonnant devinant
Il comble le réel
Et je soumets le monde dans un miroir noir
Et j'imagine ma puissance
Il fallait n'avoir rien commencé rien fini
J'efface mon image je souffle ses halos
Toutes les illusions de la mémoire
Tous les rapports ardents du silence et des rêves
Tous les chemins vivants tous les hasards sensibles
Je suis au cœur du temps et je cerne l'espace.

VII

What a beautiful spectacle indeed a beautiful spectacle
to banish. Its perfect visibility
blinds me.

From the chrysalis of my eyes
my dark double will be born
speaking against the light suspicious guessing
he crowds the real
and I submit the world in a black mirror
and I imagine my power
to have begun nothing finished nothing
I erased my image blew out its halo
all the illusions of memory
all the ardent meetings of silence and dreams
all the living pathways the tender risks
I am at the heart of time and I surround space.

VIII

Hésité et perdu succomber en soi-même
Table d'imagination calcule encore
Tu peux encore tendre tes derniers pièges
De la douleur de la terreur
La chute est à tes pieds mordre c'est devant toi
Les griffes se répandent comme du sang
Autour de toi.
Voici que le déluge sort sa tête de l'eau
Sort sa tête du feu
Et le soleil noue ses rayons cherche ton front
Pour te frapper sans cesse
Pour te voler aux nuits
Beaux sortilèges impuissants
Tu ne sais plus souffrir
Tu recules insensible invariable concret
Dans l'oubli de la force et de toutes ses formes
Et ton ombre est une serrure.

VIII

Floundering and left to sink into oneself
the imagination table still calculates
you are still able to lay your final traps
of pain of terror
the fall is at your feet the bite is before you
the claws spill as if from blood
around you.
Here as the flood draws its head from the water
pulls its mind from the fire
as the sun twists its rays looking for your face
in order to strike you ceaselessly
in order to steal you into the night
beautiful impotent spells
You no longer know how to suffer
You recoil unfeeling unchanging concrete
into the oblivion of power and all its forms
and your shadow is a lock.

II

II

I

Une vaste retraite horizons disparus
Un monde suffisant repaire de la liberté
Les ressemblances ne sont pas en rapport
Elles se heurtent.

Toutes les blessures de la lumière
Tous les battements des paupières
Et mon cœur qui se bat
Nouveauté perpétuelle des refus
Les colères ont prêté serment
Je lirai bientôt dans tes veines
Ton sang te transperce et t'éclaire
Un nouvel astre de l'amour se lève de partout.

I

A vast retreat lost horizons
a satisfying world retires from freedom
the resemblances without rapport
clash.

All the wounds of light
all the batting of eyes
and my beating heart
endless novelty of refusals
angers have readied vows
I will soon read your veins
your blood pierces you with clarity
a new star of love rises everywhere.

II

Au premier éclat tes mains ont compris
Elles étaient un rideau de phosphore
Elles ont compris la mimique étoilée
De l'amour et sa splendeur nocturne
Gorge d'ombre où les yeux du silence
S'ouvrent et brûlent.

II

In the first burst your hands understood
they were a phosphorous curtain
they understood the sparkling mimic
of love and its nocturnal splendor
shadowy gorge where silent eyes
open and offer themselves to flames.

III

Vivante à n'en plus finir
Ou morte incarnation de la mémoire
De ton existence sans moi.

Je me suis brisé sur les rochers de mon corps
Avec un enfant que j'étranglais
Et ses lèvres devenaient froides
En rêve.

D'autres ont les yeux cernés
Gelés impurs et pourrissants
Dans un miroir indifferent
Qui prend les morts pour habituels.

III

Living toward no end
or dead incarnation of memory
of your life without me.

I shattered myself on the rocks of my body
with a child that I was strangling
its lips grew cold
in a dream.

Others have circles under their eyes
frozen impure and rotting
in an indifferent mirror
that takes the dead for granted.

IV

Les espoirs les désespoirs sont effaces
Les règnes abolis les tourments les tourmentes
Se coiffent de mépris
Les astres sont dans l'eau la beauté n'a plus d'ombres
Tous les yeux se font face et des regards égaux
Partagent la merveille d'être en dehors du temps.

IV

Hopes and despairs are erased
rules abolished the torments the tempests
ready themselves with contempt
stars are in the water beauty no longer has any shadows
all eyes confront equal regard
share the wonder of being outside time.

V

Ce que je te dis ne me change pas
Je ne vais pas du plus grand au plus petit
Regarde-moi
La perspective ne joue pas pour moi
Je tiens ma place
Et tu ne peux pas t'en éloigner.

Il n'y a plus rien autour de moi
Et si je me détourne rien est à deux faces
Rien et moi.

V

What I tell you doesn't change me
I don't move from the largest to the smallest
look at me
point of view doesn't work for me
I hold my place
and you are unable to pull yourself away.

There is no longer anything around me
if I stray there is nothing on either side
nothing and me.

VI

Ma mémoire bat les cartes
Les images pensent pour moi
Je ne peux pas te perdre
C'est la fleur du secret
Un incendie à découvrir
Des yeux se ferment sur tes épaules
La lumière les réunit.

L'aile de la vue par tous les vents
Étend son ombre par la nuit
Et nul n'y pense nul n'en rêve
Et les esclaves vivent très vieux
Et les autres inventent la mort
La mort tombe mal inconceivable
Ils font du suicide un besoin
Des êtres immobiles s'ensevelissent
Dans l'espace qui les détruit
Ils envahissent la solitude
Et leur corps n'a plus de forme.

Dans les ramures hautes
Tous les oiseaux et leur forêt
Ils refusent au son ses mille differences
Les grands airs du soleil ne leur en imposent pas
Le silence supprime les grâces de saison.
Ce verre sur le marbre noir
Un seul hiver incassable
A enfermer

VI

My memory shuffles its cards
images think for me
I am unable to lose you
this is the flower of the secret
a fire to discover
eyes closed on your shoulders
light reunites them.

The wing of sight in every wind
extends its shadow by night
and nothing thinks nothing dreams
and the slaves live a long time
and others invent death
and death falls inconceivably ill
they make suicide necessary
immobile beings bury themselves
in a space that destroys them
they invade solitude
and their bodies lose their shape.

In the higher branches
all the birds and their forest
deny sound its thousand differences
the greatness of the sun doesn't impose it on them
silence suppresses the grace of the season
This glass on the black marble
one unbreakable winter
encloses

Avec l'aube aux yeux de serpent
Qui se dresse solitaire
Sur le sperme des premiers jours
Les feux noyés du verre

A calculer
La sécheresse des îles de dimension
Que mon sang baigne
Elles sont conçues à la mesure de la rosée
A la mesure du regard limpide
Dont je les nargue.

Il y a des sources sur la mer
Dans les bateaux qui me ramènent
Et des spectacles en couleurs
Dans les désastres à face humaine
J'ai fait l'amour en dépit de tout
L'on vit de ce qu'on n'apprend pas
Comme une abeille dans un obus
Comme un cerveau tombant de haut
De plus haut.
La pâleur n'indique rien c'est un gouffre
Que ne puis-je écrire
Les lettres sont mon ignorance
Entre les lettres j'y suis.
Au néant des explorateurs
Des rébus et des alphabets
Avec le clin d'œil imbecile
Des survivants que rien n'étonne
Ils sont trop je ne peux leur donner
Qu'une nourriture empoisonnée.

With dawn in the serpent's eyes
stands alone
on the sperm of the first days
the twisted fires of the glass

To calculate
the dryness of large islands
that my blood bathes
they are conceived in the measure of dew
the measure of the limpid regard
with which I flout them.

There are some springs on the sea
in the boats that bring me back
and colorful spectacles
in disasters with human faces
I made love in spite of it all
we live from that which we don't learn
like a bee in an artillery shell
like a brain falling from on high
from the highest.
pallor indicates nothing it is an abyss
I am unable to write
letters are my ignorance
between the letters I exist.
In the nothingness of explorers
of the rebus and alphabets
with the blink of the imbecilic eye
nothing astonishes the survivors
they are such that I am only able to give them
poisoned food.

La nuit simple me sert à te chercher à me guider
Parmi tous les échos d'amour qui me répondent
Personne
Sans bégayer.

The simple night serves my search for you to guide me
among all the echoes of love that respond to me
none
without stammering.

VII

Receleuse du reel
La crise et son rire de poubelle
Le crucifiement hystérique
Et ses sentiers brûlés
Le coup de cornes du feu
Les menottes de la durée
Le toucher masqué de pourriture
Tous les bâillons du hurlement
Et des supplications d'aveugle
Les pieuvres ont d'autres cordes à leur arc
D'autres arcs-en-ciel dans les yeux.

Tu ne pleureras pas
Tu ne videras pas cette besace de poussière
Et de félicités
Tu vas d'un concret à un autre
Par le plus court chemin celui des monstres.

VII

Fence for the real
crisis and laughter from a trash can
crucifyingly hysterical
and its burning pathway
the sounding horns of fire
the shackles of duration
the touch masked in rot
all the muzzled screams
and blind supplications
octopi have other cords in their arc
other rainbows in their eyes.

You will not cry
you will not empty this beggar's wallet of dust
and bliss
you are going from one concrete to another
on the shortest route that of monsters.

VIII

Tu réponds tu achèves
Le lourd secret d'argile
De l'homme tu le piétines
Tu supprimes les rues les buts
Tu te dresses sur l'enterré
Ton ombre cache sa raison d'être
Son néant ne peut s'installer.

Tu réponds tu achèves
J'abrège.
Car tu n'as jamais dit que ton dernier mot.

VIII

You respond you finish
the heavy clay secret
of the man you trample
you cancel the roads the goals
you dress yourself over the interred
your shadow hides its meaning
its nothingness cannot settle in.

You respond you finish
I cut you short
because you have never said anything but your
      final word.

IX

J'en ai pris un peu trop à mon aise
J'ai soumis des fantômes aux règles d'exception
Sans savoir que je devais les reconnaître tous
En toi qui disparais pour toujours reparaître.

IX

I took a little too comfortably
I subjected phantoms to rules of exception
without knowing that I should have recognized them all
in you who vanish always to reappear.

Stuart Kendall previously edited and co-translated two volumes of essays by Georges Bataille, *The Unfinished System of Nonknowledge* and *The Cradle of Humanity*. His other book-length translations include Jean Baudrillard's *Utopia Deferred* and Maurice Blanchot's *Lautréamont and Sade*. He is the author of a critical biography of Georges Bataille as well as articles and reviews in the fields of poetics and visual culture. He currently lives in Lexington, Kentucky.

All Black Widow Press titles are printed on acid-free paper and bound into a sewn and glued binding. Manufactured in the United States of America.

www.blackwidowpress.com

This book was set in Agfa's Rotis, designed by Otl Aicher as a modern font family that would be extremely flexible; the font is named after the village in the Allgäu where he lived. The titling font is Aculida, a modernistic typeface used by many of the Dadaists in their typographic artworks.

typeset & designed by Windhaven Press
www.windhaven.com